PIANO · VOCAL · GUITAR

INGRID MICHAELSON

IT DOESN'T HAVE
TO MAKE SENSE

ISBN 978-1-4950-7374-8

7777 W. BLUEMOUND RD. P.O. BOX 13819 MILWAUKEE, WI 53213

In Australia Contact:
Hal Leonard Australia Pty. Ltd.
4 Lentara Court
Cheltenham, Victoria, 3192 Australia
Email: ausadmin@halleonard.com.au

Visit Hal Leonard Online at
www.halleonard.com

LIGHT ME UP

Words and Music by INGRID MICHAELSON,
KATIE HERZIG and CASON COOLEY

Recorded a half step lower.

WHOLE LOT OF HEART

Words and Music by INGRID MICHAELSON,
KATIE HERZIG and CASON COOLEY

MISS AMERICA

Words and Music by INGRID MICHAELSON,
JENNY OWEN YOUNGS, LARRANCE DOPSON
and RYAN STOCKBRIDGE

ANOTHER LIFE

Words and Music by
INGRID MICHAELSON

I REMEMBER HER

Words and Music by
INGRID MICHAELSON

DRINK YOU GONE

Words and Music by INGRID MICHAELSON
and busbee

HELL NO

Words and Music by INGRID MICHAELSON,
LUKE LAIRD and BARRY DEAN

*Recorded a half step lower.

STILL THE ONE

Words and Music by INGRID MICHAELSON,
KATIE HERZIG and CASON COOLEY

CELEBRATE

Words and Music by INGRID MICHAELSON,
LUKE LAIRD and BARRY DEAN

OLD DAYS

Words and Music by INGRID MICHAELSON,
BARRY DEAN and TRENT DABBS